A **QUEER** COMPANION

a rough guide to gay slang

ABSON BOOKS LONDON

5 Sidney Square London E1 2EY England

Grateful thanks to Andrew Billington, Roger Clarke, Keith Grey, Anis Janmohamed, Bode Lawal, John Parke, Louise Quinn, Stefano Scheggi, Simon Su, Graham Ward, Roger Westwood and Sharon Elise Wright.

Edited by M. J. Ellison and Charles T. Fosberry

First published in Great Britain, May 1996

ISBN - 0 902920 960

INTRODUCTION

WHETHER gay or just gay-friendly, when taking their first steps into the homosexual world, many people find themselves confronted by codes and patterns of behaviour which seem intended to exclude new-comers. Language, whose purpose must surely be communication, can be seen rather ironically as a means of excluding others. This slim volume is intended to help anyone who has been mystified by gay slang.

The words and phrases which we as gay people use when talking to and about each other are often original and graphically amusing. One of the aims of this book is to capture these elements without losing the vibrancy of the language in the attempt.

The selection that follows inevitably reflects the author's predilections and prejudices, and if any voice has been underrepresented or indeed misrepresented we will endeavour to remedy this in a future edition.

AIDS

Acquired Immune Deficiency Syndrome, known to the ever homophobic tabloid press as the Gay Plague. Known in Africa (and elsewhere) as "Slim".

ASS/ARSE

A small selection of the vast range of synonyms: love buns, hot cross buns, cupcakes, English muffins, Dutch dumplings, bum (as in bandit), back porch, tookers. Is it a coincidence that an abundance of these terms dwell on the edible nature of the item under discussion?

AUTOFELLATION

Sucking off your favourite member, also known as self-service. If you can actually do this why not get a friend to make a video and then flog it - it's got to be easier than working for a living. As you may know, this was one of Nijinsky's party pieces (the reference is to the ballet dancer and not the racehorse!)

BALLS

King Edwards, crown jewels, orbs, rocks, family jewels, diamonds, dusters.

BASKET

When a man in bathing togs patrols the beach and all eyes swivel in his direction, chances are a well-stocked basket is on parade. Alternatives include lunch box, packet, pencil-case (for the less impressively endowed) and hamper (for the more impressively endowed).

BEAR

A particular type of gay man, whose characteristics may include being heavy, hairy, balding, older .... Rather like one's favourite uncle, only raunchier. For Bears and Bear fanciers there are specialist clubs and publications with contact ads. It must be awfully confusing, if you're actually an ursophile.

BEARD

The wife, partner or companion of a gay or bisexual man, whose Beard is presumably intended to convince the world of his rampant heterosexuality. The now dated term 'Bearded Lady' was once used to describe any queen with actual facial follicles.

BISEXUAL

Other terms include gate-swinger, convertible, ambisextrous, AC/DC, half and half, on the fence, goes both ways, wears bifocals, shops on both sides of the street, rides side saddle.

BITCH

Term of endearment or otherwise when addressing or referring to one's dearest acquaintances. As in the greeting "How're you doing, bitch?". Also used to describe what some mean queens (but never us) do as soon as their closest friends walk out of the room.

BLOW JOB

The act of fellation. Numerous alternatives, include kneeling at the altar (especially choirboys?), knob job, gob job, gum job, getting or giving a facial and the ever popular giving head.

BOLD

Meaning cheeky, impudent, up front, or direct, as in "He's ever so bold" – a phrase much used in "Round The Horne" a BBC radio comedy of the 1960's.

BONA

> The key word for any conversation using Parlare, meaning good, attractive, beautiful, nice. In "Round the Horne", Sand and Jules' Enterprises would always include bona in their name, e.g. Bona Catering, Bona Antiques.

BOYZ

> Recent term for more scene oriented gay men, who also fulfil minimum requirements on age, body shape and sexual success. So if you are old, fat or bald you are excluded from the term and, if you're all three, then you might as well be invisible for all the attention you'll get from the boyz. Just as in the old song "No-one loves a fairy when she's 40 ...."

BUDDY

> A person who is there to help someone suffering from AIDS on a one-to-one level in a practical and/or emotional way. In other words to be a good friend. Thought to derive from "Bunky", a 19th century US military term, used to describe a fellow soldier who was required to share his bunk and other equipment.

BUTCH

Formerly used to describe a virile, masculine or straight-acting man. If used with reference to a man nowadays, it is very much with tongue in cheek. Latterly, the word butch has come to denote the rougher end of the lesbian spectrum.

BUTCH SISTER

A heterosexual male

CAMP

An exaggerated display of caricatured femininity, particularly, but not necessarily by a man. The words, "mincing" and "Screaming Queen" come unbidden to mind. The use of the word in tenting circles is much to be discouraged as it causes great confusion in the gay brother- and sister-hoods. However its use in such titles as "Carry on Camping," and "The Famous Five go Camping" are singularly opposite.

CART TART

An air steward, particularly if gay (there are apparently some who are not). Rumour has it that a Concorde steward is known as an A La Carte Tart.

CHICKEN

A boy or young man below the age of consent, as referred to by an older, gay man. No connection whatsoever with the phrase "one day his chickens will come home to roost." A more appropriate usage might be a man chatting away on the 'phone, who suddenly shrieks "Must run now luv, I've got to go and stuff the chicken." A chicken fancier could be described amongst other things as a chicken-hawk, chicken-plucker or chicken-rustler - all rather agricultural terms. Is a sun tanned American Boy Scout, a Kentucky Fried Chicken and therefore "Finger Lickin' Good?"

CINDERELLA

A less than young queen who is a little too free with the powder-puff and consequently has to be tucked up by midnight before her face runs off.

CLONE

A gay man who conforms to a particular code of dress. In the seventies and eighties, this meant moustache, tight Levis etc (à la Village People and Freddie Mercury). Now, if it means anything, it implies shorter hair, looser Levis and working men's boots, but definitely no moustache.

CLOSET

Being in the closet means to deny one's homosexuality either to oneself or more commonly to others. It is a place in which Julian Clary's outfits spend a lot of time, but which he seems never to have seen the inside of .... Of course there are those who, whilst in the closet, do manage to keep the door open.

CLUB QUEEN

An habitué of clubs. Also known as a Disco Dolly.

COCK

The male member. Given all men's fascination with their own and others' appendages, there are unsurprisingly vast numbers of synonyms eg prick, dick, willy, meat, fuck pole, love muscle, nightcrawler, pork, rammer, rupert, salami, schlong ....

COME (CUM)

Spunk, jissom (gism), cream, face cream (the cock suckers' reward), fruit juice, love juice, load (as in dump one's), man seed.

COME OUT (OF THE CLOSET)

To be open about your homosexuality. This does not mean you absolutely have to scream it from the roof-tops.

COME UP

To ejaculate into your partner during anal intercourse.

CONDOM

Alternatives: rubber, rubber goods, johnny, sheath, raincoat ....

CONFIRMED BATCHELOR

A euphemism for homosexuality, a variant on "not the marrying kind" or the obituarist's favourite "he was unmarried and lived quietly with his mother".

COTTAGE

Put out of your mind any thoughts of twee thatch with roses round the front door. The reality of cruising in public toilets is a lot less picturesque and maybe that's why it has always been so popular. Fully covered in the playwright Joe Orton's Diaries and more recently in Oscar Moore's novel "A Matter of Life and Sex." The American term is tea-room.

CRUISE

The activity of seeking out like-minded souls which most of us indulge in at every opportunity - unless of course we're with our partners. Some people get a thrill from doing this at the most unlikely times, such as when out shopping with their mother.

CURRY QUEEN

A white, gay man who carries a torch for gentlemen (or otherwise) ethnically from the Indian sub-continent.

DICKLESS TRACY

Someone who isn't quite as much of a man as he would like others to believe.

DINGE QUEEN

A white whose interest lies solely in blacks. It is strongly recommended that you exercise considerable caution when using this racist phrase or others such as Coal-Burner and Midnight Queen.

DIZZY QUEEN

A favourite way of describing, hopefully with affection, one's sillier or less worldly friends. In America know as Twinky - after the famous chocolate bar.

DOCTOR MARTINS (DMs)

The obligatory footwear at the more public gay events, such as Gay Pride or shopping in Covent Garden's Tesco Metro. First made popular by the skinheads in the 60s and 70s. Other boots come into fashion, as Caterpillars did in the 90s, but only DMs are forever pink.

DOLLY DOMESTIC

When you give up roaming the streets like a rampant tiger in search of raw flesh and snuggle up on the sofa looking through the IKEA catalogue with your established partner, this is what you are. Not to be confused with Dolly Soapsuds - a laundryman in the Merchant Navy.

DRAG

The practise (or rather Art) of wearing the clothes and wildly exaggerating the characteristics of the opposite sex, usually for the sake of public display.

DRAG QUEEN

    The stars in the firmament of the gay scene. Famous/current practitioners include Danny La Rue, Lily Savage, Ruby Venezuela, Rupaul, Yvette .... Whilst drag acts are to be found regularly in many clubs and pubs around the country, Madame JoJo's in Soho is seemingly the most famous club/bar devoted solely to drag.

DRAMA QUEEN

    A term which has slipped out of the gay world and into the straight, referring to those who insist upon making a drama out of a crisis and turning mole hills into mountains.

DRAW THE BLINDS

    Pull back the foreskin. Alternatives include draw the drapes and open the Coliseum curtains.

DROP HAIRPINS

    Give hints about one's homosexuality without actually proclaiming it.

DYKE

A lover of women. Like queer this once pejorative term has been "reclaimed" by the Lesbian Movement. Alternatives include Diesel (the rougher type), Dutch girl, pansy without a stem and a vegetable (ie not a fruit).

E QUEEN

One of the many benefits of being gay is that if you indulge in a spot of Ecstasy you get called an E Queen rather than an E Head.

EEK

Parlare for face, as in Barbra's incomparable film "Funny Eek" - not forgetting Helen and her "eek that launched a thousand ships." From Ecaf, backslang for face.

FABULOSO/FANTABULOSA

This exemplifies not only the Italian origins of Parlare, but also the habit of titivating words with frilly suffixes. Thus fabulous to fabuloso, troll to trollette (walk).

FAG HAG

There are few women who would happily describe themselves as fag hags, but most gay men have women friends who, for one reason or another, enjoy the company of gay men. Alternatives include Fruit Fly and Queen Bee. What would be the equivalent for a dyke's groupie?

FAGGOT

A male homosexual. Like queer, faggot was formerly derogatory, but has now been partially reclaimed. According to the poet Roger Clarke, it is of 18th Century Hampshire origin and denotes a silly and skittish young girl. While we're at it lets air some of the other more or less offensive terms such as battyboy, bender, bum bandit, bum boy, fairy, fag, fruit, fudge-packer, marmite-driller, mary, molly, nancy, nelly, pansy, poof(ter), queen, screamer, shirtlifter, whoopsie, yoo-hoo.

FELTCH

In these safer sex days, a presumably unusual activity involving sucking one's ejaculate out of one's partner's posterior and introducing it to his mouth. Alternatively and less prissily, sucking your cum from his bum and finding another orifice to dump it in. Are there special straws for the purpose?

FEMME

The kind of dyke, also known as a Lipstick Lesbian, who does not sport the cropped hair and DMs. The terms Butch and Femme carry that rather old-fashioned heterosexual notion that gay relationships mimic straight ones by always having a dominant male and a submissive female. As if that's ever even been true of straight partnerships!

FIST

Those who find anal intercourse just a touch tame have been known to insert more substantial members into their partner's orifice, namely a fist or arm. For the more adventurous reader who wants to know more, try Larry Kramer's "Faggots."

FREEDOM FLAG

With its rainbow colours, the Freedom Flag is now generally accepted throughout the gay world as the rallying call - "Say it Loud, we're Out and Proud", much as the Pink Triangle is.

FUCK BUDDY

Someone with whom one has a relationship which is based purely on sex rather than on friendship or love.

GARDENING

Cruising in the open spaces. In London, favourite "Gardens" include Hampstead Heath, Russell Square, Holland Park, Brompton Cemetery and the South Bank. In fact, virtually any open space you care to mention, come rain or shine, as long as there is a shrubbery to disappear into. It says quite a lot about the perverse gay psyche that pansies go gardening when straights have long since hung up their hoes.

GAY

See Faggot

GET HER!

Exclamation by one queen, drawing attention to another. "Get her! Who does she think she is ...."

GIRLS' NAMES

Time was when we all had a friend who rechristened his gay male friends with girl's names eg: Tina for Christopher, Edna for Edward, Samantha for Sam. The more esoteric, old fashioned or Hollywood glam the better, such as Carmen, Gertie, Daisy.

GLORY HOLE

Ever wondered why there always seems to be a hole at about groin level between the cubicles in mens' toilets? Well, they are glory holes and they weren't put there by Mother Nature - they're totally man-made and indeed, like Kleenex tissues, they're man-sized (or not, which can be a touch disappointing).

GOLDEN SHOWER

Why bother with all those exotic shower gels in your search for that ultimate shower experience. Why not pour lager down a friend's throat and get him or her to give you his or her best shot. It's thrilling and cheap - but of doubtful nutritious value, though apparently good for the complexion. Related terms include champagne fountain and soda-fountain queen.

GRAND CANYON

An arse so slack that it's like throwing a sausage up Regent Street or down the Mersey Tunnel.

HANDKERCHIEF CODE

An unspoken language used to signal sexual preferences to potential partners. Worn in the back pocket, left is for giving and right is for getting.

Beige	Rimming	Maroon	Menstruation
Black	S & M	Navy Blue	Fucking
Brown	Shitting	Olive	Military
Chamois	Bikers	Orange	Everything
Green	Rent	Red	Fisting
Lavender	Drag	Yellow	Pissing
Light Blue	Cock-sucking		

HELIUM LEGS

One who all too readily "assumes the position". An easy lay.

HIV MAFIA

That group of predominantly gay men working in the "HIV Industry". There are reputedly two employed professionals for every person with the Virus.

ICONS

Katherine Hepburn, Madonna, Barbra Streisand, Shirley Bassey, Bette Middler, Audrey Hepburn, Dusty Springfield, Judy Garland, Marlene Dietrich, Martina Navratilova .... What do all these women have in common other than great talent? Yes, a gay following, which is the best asset that any "icon in the making" can acquire. Such fans will be loyal, supportive, passionate, generous, clean, well-dressed, nice to their mothers and will also be able to recite all the words of her songs and films at the slightest invitation. But a word of warning to the wise: biting the hand that feeds you is not a good career move - whatever did happen to Donna Summer?

INTERNET

Tired of cruising the bars, well why not surf the Internet and do a little "Virtual" Cruising - with its discussion groups, organisations, dating and escort services, mailing lists, directories and guides. The ultimate in safe sex – you can't hear or see let alone touch or smell each other. The future of sex in the 21st century?

LABEL QUEEN

Those gays who insist upon visibly displaying the power of the Pink Pound through the ruthless pursuit of designer clothes and accessories (excessories?). Stand still in Harvey Nichols' contemporary menswear department of a Saturday afternoon, and a pound to a penny you will be mown down by a couple of Label Queens in less than a flutter of an eyelash. Also known as Tag Hags.

LADY OF LEISURE

A kept queen with time on her hands; and you know what Mother said about the Devil finding work for idle hands.

LALLIES

Parlare for legs, as in "Vada the bona lallies!"

LATTY

Home or house in Parlare. "There's nantiwhere like latty, sweet latty."

LEATHER QUEEN

Just because he has a wardrobe full of leather it doesn't mean he has a motorbike in the garage.

LEVIS

Every self-respecting queer has at least one pair. The rougher and more abused looking the better, but then that's true of many gay men's taste in men – as well as jeans. If there were a sudden outbreak of the Denim Weevil goodness knows what we would all wear.

LOST AT SEA

Being "driven" to homosexuality by long confinement with only one's own sex for comfort. A likely story, I don't think.

LUBE

Lubricant for sex - hopefully a water-based lubricant (like KY jelly) when used in conjunction with rubber. To lube up is to apply lubrication.

LUNCHBOX

Crotch, packet, basket, jewel-case. There's nothing like a well packed lunch-box to make a picnic go with a swing.

MASTURBATE

Everyone has their own particular favourite, but here are a few: beat the meat, flog (also flog the log), bang the bishop, toss off, five finger exercise, wank, fuck the fist, jack off, jerk off, pull (the pudding/pud) and wave the wand - after all every fairy has a wand.

MEAT- RACK

Traditionally a place for picking up male prostitutes or rent (boys), such as any amusement arcade where chicken is on the menu. Also refers to bars or clubs where heavy cruising occurs.

MINCE/MINCING

To walk in an openly (not to say provocatively) effeminate way. Used disparagingly or jokily about the way certain gay men walk "Get her, mincing down the street like Mae West". An alternative is to swish.

MOTSS

An Internet abbreviation for Members Of The Same Sex

MUSCLE MARY

One who spends an inordinate amount of time at the gym (hence Gym Queen) supposedly for the purpose of exercise. Any lengthy periods spent in the showers and changing rooms are purely co-incidental.

NANTE/NANTI

The negative and the very antithesis of Bona in Parlare. "Bona lallies she may have, but vada the riah - nante!"

OMIPALONE

Man or boy in Parlare. See Palone.

OPEN ONE'S PURSE

To break wind, to fart.

OUT

To expose a public figure as gay. A somewhat controversial activity which divides the gay community. Also describes a person who is out of the closet.

PALONE

A woman or girl in Parlare, as in Hepburn's famous film "My Fair Palone". See Omipalone.

PARLARE

A language/slang from the 1940s used by gays so that they could converse secretly in public. With the rise of Gay Liberation in the 1960s it tended to drop out of use. The code was broken to a limited extent in the radio series "Round the Horne" and "Beyond our Ken".

PINK

The shade deemed by Society to be the gay colour. Now enshrined as such by gays - hence pink triangles, The Pink Paper, the pink pound and of course The Pink Panther (with a waist that thin he has to be gay).

POTATO QUEEN
Someone with a taste for the Irish.

PRIDE/GAY PRIDE
The time of year in all enlightened cities of the world when gay men and women take to the streets to be out, loud and proud. With each passing year the party gets bigger.

QUEEN
A term for a gay man, but more frequently used to denote a more effeminate member of the fraternity. No connection with the Queen Mary (a ship), Queen Elizabeth (a monarch - or two) or the Queen of Puddings (anyone you know?).

QUEER
A derogatory term for gays used by heterosexuals. Now "reclaimed" by the gay community so as to take the sting from the term. See also Faggot.

QUEER STREET

Old Compton Street is the nearest London comes to having the equivalent of Sydney's Oxford Street or San Francisco's Castro. And London's not the only British city with a recognised gay area: Manchester's Canal Street, Birmingham's Hurst Street and Brighton's St James Street in Kemp Town.

RENT-BOY

Young, male prostitute.

RIAH

Parlare for hair - a good example of backslang. Fake riah - a wig or toupee.

RICE QUEEN

A specialist in men with Eastern (or more particularly Oriental) promise.

RIM/REAM

To lick or tongue the anus. Enough said!

RUBBER UP

To put on a condom

S & M (SADO-MASOCHISM)

Once thought to be the preserve of the truly depraved, this corner of the sexual playground has now become part of the mainstream - witness the imagery used in music videos by such artists as Madonna.

SAFER SEX

There being no such thing as "safe" sex, the term "safer" sex is being used to encourage the use of condoms in both penetrative and oral sex.

SAINT DEREK (OF DUNGENESS)

Derek Jarman (1942-1994) was canonised by the Sisters of Perpetual Indulgence as their first gay saint in recognition of his work as an artist, film-maker, author and gardener, all of which openly reflected his homosexuality.

SCENE QUEEN

Frequenters of the clubs, bars, restaurants and streets which are considered to be the centre of the gay world. Hence Club Queen and Queen of Clubs.

SEAFOOD

A member of the Royal Navy, a sailor. As the song says "there's something about a sailor..." And remember Frutte de Mare might not always be a way of describing a lobster. Perhaps a soupçon nastily, a woman with a sailor boyfriend is called a Seacow.

SIMILES

A few favourites:

Camp as a row of tents

As gay as a goose (why goose for Heaven's sake?)

As queer as a coot (Coote) – after 18c cause célèbre (Sir Eyre Coote caught spanking a bunch of school boys)

As bent as a boomerang (or fish-hook)

As queer as a clockwork mouse (or orange)

SISTERS OF PERPETUAL INDULGENCE

Originating in San Francisco in the 1970s, an order of male "nuns", whose British sisterhood includes:

Sister Frigidity of Nocturnal Emissions
Sister Melancholia than Thou
Sister Sic Transit Gloria Swansong
Sister Moses of the Parting Cheeks
Sister Anorexia of the Cellulite
Sister of the Immaculate Deception
Blessed Easy Access of the Chapped Orifice
Reverend Mother Suxcox

SIZE QUEEN

One whose prime requirement when choosing a partner is a large Membrum Virile (or lunch-box if you failed your Latin Primer and cannot remember Simon Callow's lecture with diagram in the opening sequence of the film Maurice).

SLUT

Whilst it might be politically incorrect to call a straight woman a slut, try shouting the term at the top of your voice in any gay club and you're sure to get a few hundred men to respond in unison.

SMALLADS / CLASSIFIEDS

Some abbreviations which may be of use.

ALAWP	all letters answered with photo
CBT	cock and ball torture
CP	corporal punishment
DIY	do it yourself (masturbation)
DM	Doc Martin wearer
FF	Fist fucking
gdlk	good-looking
GSOH	good sense of humour
JO	jack/jerk off
S/M	sado-masochism
TT	tit torture
WLTM	would like to meet
WS	water sports (pissing)
VWE	very well endowed

See also Handkerchief Code.

SNOW QUEEN

A black man who has a preference for white men. Also know as a snow-shoveler.

SNOWBALL

Kissing after 69-ing, which involves the exchange of more bodily fluids than just saliva. Presumably in these safer sex days a less common practice than in days of yore. Remember Woody Allen's answer to the question of whether he thought sex was dirty – "Yes, if you're doing it properly."

SPAG FAG

A term (presumably derived from spaghetti) for one whose proclivities lean him in the direction of Italians.

SUPERMARKET

Who said shopping had to be dull? Well not any more. Cruising to the "Sound of Musak" has become a hobby in which many gays excel.

TBH (TO BE HAD)

A person who though not gay might, under the right circumstances, surprise themselves.

TRADE

Trade means many things to many people. A gay or possibly "straight" man who is available for casual sex. It can also allude to sexual dominance, hence Rough Trade. Queens (in the fluffy sense) cannot be trade, but might avail themselves of such. Used in the oft asked question - "What was that bit of trade I saw you with last night?"

TROLL

Parlare for walk or go. "Who do you think you are, trolling in at 3 am ....?"

TROLLEY DOLLY

An air steward. See also Cart Tart.

UP YOUR GARY GLITTER

From rhyming cockney slang - shitter or arsehole. As in "I just bent down to undo my shoelaces and he went straight up me Gary Glitter."

VADA

To look at or draw attention to in Parlare: "How nice to vada your dolly old eek again!"

WASH AND GO

Forget any thoughts of shampoo products, we are talking here about the post-orgasmic behaviour of our less romantic conquests, who depart without even pausing for a fag - let alone a hug.

YMCA (YOUNG MEN'S CHRISTIAN ASSOCIATION)

The unofficial position of this association as the focus of gay fantasy was recognised in the 1970s by the Village People's song "YMCA" .